Making
Great Decisions
Reflections

ALSO BY T.D. JAKES

Making
Great Decisions
Reflections

For a Life Without Limits

T.D. Jakes

ATRIA BOOKS

New York   London   Toronto   Sydney

ATRIA BOOKS

A Division of Simon & Schuster, Inc.
1230 Avenue of the Americas
New York, NY 10020

First Atria Books hardcover edition June 2009

ATRIA BOOKS and colophon are trademarks of Simon & Schuster, Inc.

For information about special discounts for bulk purchases, please contact Simon & Schuster Special Sales at 1-866-506-1949 or business@simonandschuster.com.

The Simon & Schuster Speakers Bureau can bring authors to your live event. For more information or to book an event, contact the Simon & Schuster Speakers Bureau at 1-866-248-3049 or visit our website at www.simonspeakers.com.

Designed by Nancy Singer

Manufactured in the United States of America

10 9 8 7 6 5 4 3 2 1

Library of Congress Cataloging-in-Publication Data

Jakes, T.D.
    Making great decisions reflections: for a life without limits / by T.D. Jakes. — 1st Atria Books hardcover ed.
        p.   cm.
    1. Mate selection.   2. Decision making.   3. Life skills.   I. Title.
HQ801.J266 2009
248.8'4—dc22   2008044355

ISBN: 978-1-4165-4753-2

I dedicate this book to my home church, The Potter's House of Dallas, to my partners in ministry—the Bishop's Circle and Aaron's Army—and to all those who understand that destiny will open its doors based on the integrity of your next few decisions. These are the words of wisdom that I believe will help you with those difficult choices before you do.

Introduction

No other choice leaves as many footprints alongside your own on life's journey as the decision to unite yourself with another person, a partner, a spouse. Realistically, marriage, and any relationship, can become joyful companionship or torturous tantrums.

Relationship decisions are like dominoes, each one toppling one irreversible consequence into another. And while we cannot scrutinize, analyze, and fantasize about each and every decision we make, we must do so for the larger, more significant relationship decisions of life. Decisions about who and when to date, court, and marry, shared lifestyle choices, and friendships demand that we bring everything we have to the table to ensure that we make the best choices and never look back.

Most of us have learned, some the hard way, the importance of relationships. But do we move into these decisions in a way that will ensure positive results?

I explore that question in depth with you in *Before You Do*. This *Reflections* book is a daily reinforcer of the ideas you encountered there. Your future is as strong as the decisions that precede it, and with practice in reframing your thinking, you can make relationship decisions with a confidence, faith, and fortitude that allow you the freedom to enjoy a contented, fulfilled life.

It's all in how you approach the decisions. In this book you will find affirming helps and self-reminders that will allow your innate, God-given sensitivity and propensity to caution to override your tendency toward emotion.

As in *Before You Do,* romantic relationships and the selection of a spouse are the core example of the book; however, the skills and information I reinforce here are not exclusively effective for seeking companionship. What you embrace and practice about decision making in this book can be applied to any area of your life, especially in protecting yourself from the highly expensive and emotionally devastating consequences of acting on impulse. And because this book of *Reflections* is on *Before You Do,* it will help you avoid losing time in procrastination (which is often caused by the fear of making the wrong decision), and will mentally prepare you for action.

All major decisions require due diligence and deliberation, whether you're choosing a husband, selecting a major in college, acquiring property, deciding on a new career, buying a company, or determining where you will live. My goal in this book of *Reflections* is to help you realize that some decisions are so significant that you want to make them with as much certainty as possible.

If you have ever wished that you could see into the future in order to make a present decision, this book won't grant you the power of prophecy, but it can help you know all you need to know to move confidently into the future. If you spend time with the Reflections in this book, you will be equipped, ready to make foolproof relational decisions, with God's grace.

How to Use This Book

This companion book to *Before You Do* is designed to be read one Reflection at a time, and thought about over and over again. It complements the key elements in *Before You Do,* and the subheadings—Before, You, and Do—are a memory device intended to help you embrace, absorb, and apply the messages of my book.

Reflection is important as you make relationship decisions. And even before you reflect, you must know what requires contemplation. Part of the process is carefully balancing your heart and mind—your emotions and your thinking—so that the resulting decision is based on your best, most true self and so that you grasp your ability to act in a new way.

The **Before** feature is the key idea you will reflect on. It is framed as a personal statement for you to meditate on, recite, and perhaps even memorize.

The **You** element is a brief text passage, also written as an "I" statement, for you to use as a yardstick for your own self-examination. It's meant for you to ponder, to spur your own fresh thinking about yourself and the decisions you are making.

The **Do** item is the short summary statement. Use it as you decide what to *do*!

The Reflection numbers are for convenience only, although they generally follow the flow of *Before You Do*. Read the Reflections in the order that fits your needs. Skip ones that don't; come back to them another time. Let the book draw you back to the pages that you need as you need them.

Making
Great Decisions
Reflections

Reflection 1

Before I take any great step OR make any decision, I must deromanticize it.

You

I have seen far too many marriages and other kinds of great beginnings that ended horrendously. My focus must be not, on the plans, but on the far more difficult processes that follow, the long-term consequences of my relationship decisions. I must see not only the face of my sweetie pie but the face I will wake up next to for the rest of my life, the face of my partner of choice, the face I will run to when life becomes cold and pains are unbearable. The one I must choose as carefully as a warrior selects a weapon or an artist selects a medium—my weapon of choice when I fight layoffs, mounting bills, pressure, and unimaginable challenge. The face I will watch convulse with the aches and pains of disease and injury; the face that will comfort me and the hand I will squeeze in sorrow.

Do

I do not romanticize my perspectives based on commercials and soap operas. Life is not always easy. I must begin to glimpse what many don't learn until they experience pain and regret.

Reflection 2

Before I choose a spouse or make any relationship decision, I must know how to deliberate carefully.

You

I must be as deliberate as possible, as logical, objective, and thoughtful in my decision to commit, cohabitate, and commingle my DNA. Love need not leave me intoxicated and blind to the realities that await me in a close relationship: bills to be paid, diapers to be changed, cars to be repaired, homes to be moved, jobs to be completed, on and on throughout all the seasons of my life. This is what I'm committing to. I'm not committing to a lifetime of good chemistry or shared ideals or that tingling feeling inside.

This reality also must not dampen my enthusiasm for a relationship, or make me cynical and suspect of the joys that married life can afford. But I must make every relationship decision with appropriate care and deliberation. So much of the rest of my life comes down to this one decision.

Do
_____

I do act based on logic, objectives, and thought—not solely emotions—in all my relationship decisions.

Reflection 3

Before I make a pivotal decision, I will examine the power of one single choice to shape the rest of my life, and the lives of others.

You

The power of one individual decision can never be underestimated. Fortunes have been gained and lost, marriages mended and torn, children born or buried, all because of one person's decision, which may have seemed of little importance at the time.

I understand that life has a way of knocking me down. My life will be easier the fewer mistakes I make. Life brings real challenges but I do not have to give way to pressure, anger, or disappointment and succumb to pain, losing sight of my passion and purpose. I realize that every important relationship decision affects the quality of my entire life.

Do

I do move into relationship decisions in a way that will ensure positive results. I will do everything I can to ensure the best choices for my life.

Reflection 4

Before I make an important relationship decision, I realize that I can't afford to make a bad choice and face a setback.

You

I have to make every move count. I do not want to have to recover economically, emotionally, or spiritually from a massive setback that could result from a bad decision.

This means that sometimes, even after I spend time and money, even invest emotionally in a relationship, I have to decide against it. Others may say, "You did all of that and still walked away?" What I spent investigating it might seem wasted to them, but not to me.

I have learned that relationship decisions come down to five crucial components:

Research—*gathering information and collecting data*

Roadwork—*removing obstacles and clearing the path*

Rewards—*listing choices and imagining their consequences*

Revelation—*narrowing my options and making my selection*

Rearview—*looking back and adjusting as necessary to stay on course*

In fact, these components can be applied to any area of my life. Whether choosing a spouse, selecting a major in college, acquiring property, deciding on a new career, buying a company, or determining where I will live, all my major decisions require due diligence and deliberation. I want to make significant decisions with as much certainty as possible. If I do, I'll move confidently into the future with no regrets.

Do
_____

I do gather as much data as possible before making a big decision.

Reflection 5

Before I credit extenuating circumstances beyond my control to my achievement or failure, I admit that I am a victim or victor of my own making, because of a key decision.

You

I can trace every success or failure in my life back to something I did or didn't decide effectively—whether in the course of developing relationships, doing business, or selecting investments, or in any other area. My decisions set the course of my life. I must put in place the necessary prerequisites to accomplish my desired goals. Past decisions and their consequences can be offset by decisions I make now.

Do

I do hold myself responsible for my life and expect good results as I exercise the process of reflection-discernment-decision.

Reflection 6

Before I make an important decision, I open myself to observations from others I trust and respect.

You

People who work with me often notice things about me that I have not realized about myself. These colleagues can make interesting observations about me. I must listen to—though perhaps not always heed—their advice, and remain approachable for feedback. They may notice tendencies in my approach to life that I don't see in myself, left only to my own thoughts.

Am I getting feedback about myself from others? This is a key question I must ask in the name of doing due diligence. I need to be armed with answers about ME before setting out to make important decisions.

I have to ask tough questions about myself and have real

answers that predict how I will manage issues, struggles, and maladies that are inherent in the normal processes of life.

Sound decisions are based on great information, so the more significant the question, the more internal due diligence and external feedback I must require of myself.

Do

I do ask the necessary questions of others to get a true picture of myself, as I reflect, discern, and decide on important matters.

Reflection 7

Before I decide, I will listen to my own inner voice.

You

I must know myself so well that I can discern my own uncertainty, know when I am trying to convince myself, even when I protest too loudly. I must know what I do and don't really *like* and what is and is not important to me.

Before choosing, I actually need to look at myself. I must self-examine, compare my competing inner desires. I must also factor in the importance of LIKING ME.

Some people make how they feel, how much they like themselves, their number one criterion for decisions. They don't consider others. While I won't go to that extreme, in order to make decisions that I will never regret, I must be willing to think through all the criteria—professional and personal, scientific and subjective, data-driven—and make a choice that is self-satisfying. Much of the anxiety and later regret that come from the weight of my decisions can be alleviated or avoided if I assemble all my information—that which is clearly consequential as well as what may *seem* inconsequential.

Do

I do listen to my heart as well as my mind.

Reflection 8

Before I gather information for my decision, I affirm that no question is too stupid to ask.

You

The first step in making life-changing decisions, even the most personal and emotional ones, without regret is research. Research fuels my choices by yielding the information on which I can base a sound decision. My choices are no stronger than the facts that I have in choosing relationships. I am not one who is easily convinced; I require concrete information before reaching a decision, because it alters the quality of my life. I would rather lengthen the deliberation process and ensure that the decision is appropriate than reach a hasty conclusion.

Like everyone, I sometimes feel intimidated as I deliberate, and I counter that feeling with this statement: It is not how much I know that arms me with the tools of great deci-sion making, but rather how much I *ask*.

I will ask questions. The most intelligent people asked questions of science, art, religion, that most others took for granted. I can never know more than I am willing to ask.

Do ─────────────

I do work hard to make my life a safe environment for in-quiry, due diligence, reflection, and problem solving, and never attempt to silence the voice within me that continues to question.

Reflection 9

Before the issues I never thought to ask about wreak havoc on my relationship, I will force the hard questions.

You

When the tingly, euphoric feelings of new love wear off—and they eventually do—I have to know who I am and who my potential mate is. Knowing things such as what kind of person they are, their character, their life goals, their moral and spiritual beliefs, whether or not they are emotionally stable and available, any health issues they might have, are all important considerations that I don't often see discussed, that aren't considered very "romantic." But these issues are, in fact, a very real part of life, and can wreak havoc on my relationship if not considered.

Do

I do make every effort to find out who my partner really is.

Reflection 10

Before I make rash and irrational decisions, I will see loneliness as a gift, solitude as my time of preparation for a good relationship.

You

Everybody needs somebody. Many people need companionship so much that they are more horrified at the thought of being alone than they are at the prospect of being unhappy. I will not be one of those people. I cannot make good relationship decisions when my decision is rooted in the fear of being alone or the fear of being rejected.

I will not be embarrassed to admit that I want someone to share my life; I won't pretend that I don't need anyone. I was created with a need for socialization. I accept myself for having that need. When I admit to being lonely or wanting to be loved, I am not being weak. There is absolutely nothing wrong with feeling that need, as long as the need does not control me or cause me to make inappropriate choices to fulfill it.

Do
_____

I do acknowledge that I may be someone who flourishes in social environments; that I need a person to support, affirm, and give me a sense of belonging; that I get a degree of gratification when I contribute to someone else's well-being, especially when my effort is appreciated.

Reflection 11

Before I blame, I take ownership of the solution.

You

I sometimes play the blame game; I respond to a situation by not taking responsibility for my role and blaming others.

Most of my life's predicaments are resolvable if I would own the issue and take responsibility, at least, for its resolve, if not for its origin. Maybe I didn't cause it, but it has fallen to my lot to decide to fix it, rather than place blame.

Do

I do accept responsibility for fixing problems even if I didn't cause them.

Reflection 12

Before I decide anything major, and as I take responsibility for my decision, I let go of self-blame.

You

I am not God. Only God has power and wisdom in every issue and action that occurs in my world. I am a participant but not the only contributing factor in my life.

It's tempting to think that these self-blaming people are better. If I take total responsibility for everything, I am just as unhealthy in my thinking as though I were negligent and unwilling to take any responsibility. Both extremes focus only on ME. Good relationship decisions can come from neither end of the spectrum.

Perhaps I don't respond in these extremes but, like most people, gravitate toward one polarity or the other when faced with hard decisions. I must admit the tough reality that I *do* play some part in the state I now find myself in, but recognize that I did not get here by myself. I can decide not to blame myself, just as I decide not to blame others, outside factors, unfair conditions, circumstances, any number of valid reasons for my relationship issues. But eventually I have to let all that blame go and do something.

Do _____

I do put aside blame and take action.

Reflection 13

Before I blame, I acknowledge it is a learned behavior that I can unlearn.

You

I can learn how to break this perpetual destructive habit. I choose to move beyond past mistakes, to develop a strategy that focuses on where I am going, what I would like to see happen. I bring healing by the admission that I have contributed to where I am now, guilty because of what I did say or do, or that I silently stood by and enabled the destructive behavior.

Positive changes will come when I move into the future and begin to visualize what success looks like, focus on what a functional situation would look like. Instead of spending energy on blame, I focus on some task based on my new vision of my life.

As I move toward goals, rather than spend too much energy affixed to the sour pathology of past relationships or former interactions, I empower myself. I get my power back.

Do _____

I do place blame behind me and focus on what success looks like.

Reflection 14

Before I take responsibility for others' lives, I solve my own challenging circumstances.

You

Sometimes I can be a "martyr"—the one who is quick to say, "Oh, poor me . . . ," and then fill in the blank. In other words: "Because I was responsible for (blank), there was no way I could do (blank) for myself." This translates as: I allowed myself to be unhappy and I am blaming others, rather than the person really responsible for my choices—me.

While the circumstances may in fact be true, the martyr in me focuses so much on other people and taking responsibility for others' lives that I don't take the time to look for solutions to my situation.

This passive approach keeps me stuck in my circumstances, attached to my self-created drama. My life is not a martyr story; woe and hard times are not my identity. I make choices in life to stay or go, to confront or ignore, to complain or look for a solution.

The most tragic by-product of martyrdom is that it absolves me of responsibility for my life, allows someone else's life to determine mine. I believe that I have the power to right the wrongs, correct the mistakes, and move forward in spite of the maladies and mishaps of the past. I can overcome insurmountable odds, even if I have been victimized by someone else's decision. I can emerge with a strategy that enables me to stop neglecting my destiny and refuse to blame my self-sacrifice for others as the reason I do not take responsibility for myself, for my situation.

Do

I do not act as a martyr.

Reflection 15

Before I choose to be angry, I make the decision to work at a solution.

You

A commandment at the foundation of making regret-free decisions: *I am the people I have been waiting for and no one else is coming.* If I own the responsibility for my life, I discover that no matter what others do or don't do to me or for me, I'm still accountable to myself. I decide how I respond. I decide to continue to move toward my dreams.

Prince Charming isn't waiting for me around the corner. My ship isn't coming in. The systems of this world have not been fair, but personal responsibility has a role beside, if not in front of, social justice. I have a choice to make. I can stand with angry fists raised, or I can assume responsibility and refuse to be a victim of my own anger.

Do
_____

I do solve the things that are within my power to change.

Reflection 16

Before I give in to feeling battered, I choose faith that I can rebuild my own life.

You

I do not yield power over my life to others. Nor do I flatter others with the admission that their sins of commission or omission leave me so traumatized that they and they alone can end my suffering. I tenaciously gather what power is within my reach—no matter how small—and rebuild my own life no matter how battered I might feel by circumstances.

While I ask for help when I need it, I do not wait for assistance. I have the power to lift myself beyond any dismal realities that I may face.

Do

I do have the power to rebuild by making sound decisions henceforth.

Reflection 17

Before anything will change, I must decide I want to change.

You

Humans were created to be leaders, innately and instinctively, exceeding any other living being. I have the power to evolve, transform, develop, relocate, rebuild, reinvent, or do whatever else is necessary to achieve my goals. But nothing will happen or change in my situation until I decide I want it to. When I'm willing to recognize the vast power I hold in the choices I make, then my life will ignite.

In the titillating, terrifying, gut-wrenching, soul-tingling feelings of this vertigo, we learn the value of faith and the fuel of prayer.

Do

I do choose to change.

Reflection 18

Before I get overwhelmed by my feelings as I undergo change, I remind myself that it is normal to feel many emotions as I make wise decisions that change my life.

You

I accept that as I take responsibility for my life and my decisions I may experience a wide range of emotions: Anger, thinking that life is unfair and that this isn't what I wanted for myself. Fear, that I will fail and have only myself to blame. Maybe I'll feel annoyed that I have to consider my life in a different light. I may even feel sad. I might feel ashamed of my past mistakes and unsure if I really can take responsibility and move forward.

Whatever emotion comes up, I know that it is normal when making changes—especially drastic ones. Regardless of how I feel, I won't judge myself. I acknowledge what I am feeling, consider whether my thoughts are rational or whether

they are just fear talking, and then I hold fast to my commitment to change.

Do
———————————

I do acknowledge my feelings but remain committed to
change.

Reflection 19

Before I make a decision, I affirm that looking at the outside of a person, relationship, or situation does not always reflect what is on the inside.

You

Jesus said about the Pharisees that outside they were clean, but inside they were full of dead men's bones (Matthew 23:27). Some people look far better on the outside than on the inside. They refuse to discard what used to be; they refuse to discard what was.

Do

I do let what has passed be past.

Reflection 20

Before the script changes, I recognize that my role stays the same.

You

When faced with significant opportunities, I may find my vision impaired by emotional and psychological baggage. Maybe I keep getting into relationships with the wrong kind of person, getting caught in a cycle of attraction that traps me in drama. My past disappointment, dysfunction, and desperation have created a script in which the actors or actresses may change, but the role they play stays the same.

Each time I start over, I carry past experiences into the new relationship.

Maybe I find myself trapped in an unhealthy workplace environment that I'm afraid to leave. Because of past experiences, I can't see beyond the short-term need for a paycheck. My vision of a broader professional panorama becomes eclipsed by my feelings of inferiority, inadequacy, and incompetency. I postpone decisions about going back to school and finishing my degree, looking into other career fields, or asking my supervisor about a promotion.

I am going to make great decisions that leave me with no regrets, so I must let go of the past. Doing so will provide me the necessary space to see, breathe, and maneuver.

Do

I do let go of old baggage, and clear the mental and emotional room to experience the here and now.

Reflection 21

Before I can see the beauty in my surroundings, I must remove the clutter.

You

I have grown attached to some things that I don't need but lack the courage or resolve to release. Whether my malaise is because I am still grieving over a death, a divorce, or another traumatic change in my life, if the things I'm holding on to threaten my well-being and stifle my life, I need to remove all trash, clutter, and items that are beyond repair. The removal of unneeded items can reveal the beauty, functionality, and lovely features of my home. This simple act will reinforce for me that I can "clean house" and start fresh, and it will confirm my desire to change. And there is no greater avenue for change in my life than exercising the very real power I have each and every day to execute decisions different from the ones that got me where I am now.

Do _____

I do unclutter.

Reflection 22

Before emotional junk weighs me down, I learn to let go of negative feelings.

You

Mental and emotional junk are the regrets I have about past mistakes, the grudges I hold when I feel I've been done wrong, or the hurts I hide under clouds of anger, cynicism, and re- clusiveness. Mental and emotional junk weigh me down. When I hold grudges or hang on to past mistakes, even my own, I feel heavy, encumbered.

My relationships can't flourish when I haven't processed my mental junk. Like blame, mental junk keeps me stuck in the past. If an old beau has hurt me, and I've never let that hurt go, each time my mate does something similar, I react, probably with unwarranted fervor, as if he were the original person who hurt me. The new mate is rightfully upset and confused at my over-the-top reaction to a small infraction.

Just as I have to keep my home free of physical junk, I have to focus on keeping my mental and emotional "house" clean and in order as well. Praying, journaling, meditation, and exercise are common ways to be sure my emotional issues of the past aren't seeping into my current relationships. These activities help me remain on top of and aware of my emotions and feelings, rather than stuffing them inside.

When issues do come up, I commit myself to talk them through in kindness, truth, and honesty.

Do _____

I do keep my emotional house in order.

Reflection 23

Before I free my soul from the past, I must forgive others.

You

I accept the challenge to look in my emotional closets and see what needs clearing out. If I have dead relationships lingering, I let them go. I move on. I make room for new life. New life requires removing items, relationships, and obligations that no longer serve the purpose for which they were originally intended.

No one but me knows what is in my mind, my feelings. I clean out old memories that attract unforgiveness, anything that keeps my heart filled with anger, hostility, and bitterness. I give myself the gift of forgiveness. Through this, I unhook myself from the past and free my soul to escape the dismal and experience the delightful again.

This is a moment in my life when I discard the ills that

afflict me. I have the power to do this because there is more life in front of me than there is behind me!

Do ────────────

I do forgive old wrongs, discard old hurts, and make room for a new life.

Reflection 24

Before I break negative cycles, I affirm that I can change, no matter how many mistakes I've made.

You

I do not have to stay tied to past mistakes for the rest of my life. Breaking these kinds of cycles—repeated mistakes—requires making a decision. It doesn't matter how many mistakes I've made, how traumatic the circumstances from which I have come, or how distant I feel from the childhood dreams that once motivated me; if I want to change, I can.

I want to move on with my life. It won't happen overnight and it won't be easy, but I have an insatiable desire for a better life that gnaws at me and I will take action. I have decided to do so.

I will not wait for a health crisis, job termination, or loss of a loved one to act on my desire for lasting change. I look into my past without fear, blame, shame, anger, bitterness, or self-reproach. I am becoming the person God created me to be.

I will find a way to move out of the past, and move ahead, free of all encumbrances that threaten to leave me attached to the past.

I will not allow my unwillingness to forgive, my bitterness, or any other deep scar to dictate my future.

Do
_____

I do not let dead weight impede my progress.

Reflection 25

Before I move forward, some things just need to be put back where they belong.

You

Some relationships need to be severed. Others may require some closure for me to move on. Still others simply need to be put back in their proper place. Finally, some aren't going away but I can contain them. I can set healthy relationship boundaries to ensure that they are not consuming space in my life that is reserved for others and for myself.

Once I've eliminated or set boundaries on relationships, I can begin to reassess my needs and maintain only those relationships that I choose—those that are useful and helpful for my journey.

My prayer: Holy Spirit, please clean out my heart, make over my soul, and allow me to get rid of the accumulated things that diminish me as an individual, as an employee, or as a lover.

Do _____

I do put things in their proper place, and I am not afraid for someone to look in my heart, because I have gotten rid of what might have limited or embarrassed me.

Reflection 26

Before I become the CEO of my life, I examine who makes decisions about my life.

You

God is the owner of my "team" but gave me authority to run it. I have power and dominion in my life. God owns my life, but I care for it. This gives me the power to make the necessary decisions in my life and moves me from victimhood to being a victor. The great decisions are mine to make. I alone have the responsibility to make the choices that will affect my own performance, productivity, and profitability. I have stakeholders and shareholders, those that support me and those that compete with me. At the end of the day, it is me, the CEO of my life, sitting in my corner office, who is responsible for the bottom line. I will guide my life and reap the dividends for which I was created.

Do
_____

I do take leadership of my life.

Reflection 27

Before I try to "do it all," I draw on other people's strengths to help me succeed.

You

I surround myself with others who complement my strengths and compensate for my weaknesses. I am still in charge, but I have people available working on my side to help me succeed. I work together with others, focusing on my strengths and acknowledging my weaknesses.

In areas where I need more support, or face challenges that don't fall into the realm of my strengths, I call on my team members to use their skills to help me out.

Do

I do ask for help in my weak areas.

Reflection 28

Before I can fully lead, I must withstand controversy and conflict.

You

I begin the process now of examining myself and choosing the kind of leader I want to be. Leaders have four characteristics:

Leaders tend to be controversial.

Leaders' decisions create conflict.

Leaders are persons of commitment.

Leaders are guided by their character.

I accept being controversial. Many people will not accept where I'm going until after I get there. I commit to being tolerant of conflict. I cannot wait until every conflict is resolved to proceed. I affirm that I am a person of commitment and character. I remain flexible, nimble, and adaptable to changes.

When family members no longer support my dream, when my spouse doesn't encourage my passion, when my kids require more of me, I refuse to enter a spiral of discouragement, depression, or diversion, and I forge onward.

Do
_____

I do handle controversy and conflict, and am a person of commitment and character.

Reflection 29

Before I lead, I set boundaries.

You

I need to maintain firm boundaries; otherwise, people will attempt to derail my dream. I am learning when to say "No." I know that it's okay to walk away alone with my head held high rather than to conform to someone else's standard of who I should be.

I understand that no one, even those who love me most, can pursue my goals the way I can. I do not need to resort to shortcuts to achieve my goals. I cultivate integrity, playing by the rules, working hard, and giving others credit when it's due. I live by faith. I trust my Creator to help me accomplish all that I was made and called to do.

Do

I do have the character to set boundaries as a leader.

Reflection 30

Before I decide, I accept that not everyone will be pleased with every decision I make.

You

I step up and take responsibility as the leader of my life, knowing that plenty of people will be more than willing to sit back and critique everything I do. I won't let these people deter me from my success. I commit to treating everyone with courtesy and respect, but I will not worry about individuals who focus on petty, negative issues.

Even within my family, not everyone is going to be happy with my decisions. My job is to lead in a way that is best for me, and the whole family. I will make the right decision, popular or not.

Do

I do not let petty, negative complainers deter me from success.

Reflection 31

Before I select my "team," I get clear on who are confidants, constituents, and comrades.

You

Some people come into my life for a season and others for a lifetime. I do not attempt to make seasonal people lifetime participants.

Confidants are people in my life for the long haul. They are there for a lifetime, offering unconditional acceptance. In the span of my life, I do not expect many of these secret-keepers. With no ulterior motives, they will be there because they are drawn to me and want to be there for me. I can rest in the security of such relationships, to express myself and glean wise counsel.

Constituents walk with me because they share my goals. They agree to principles on which I've based my life. They are with me for the common goals, and as long as it serves their purpose, they will travel as part of my team. I accept that they will hitch another ride if they decide they can get there faster or better with another driver. I need constituents for the energy and passion they often contribute to my life, but I won't love constituents or mistake them for confidants, because I know they're not here for *me*—they're here for what we have in common.

Comrades are not for me, nor do we have much in common. They're attracted to me because they're fighting what I'm fighting. Comrades galvanize around common enemies. When the fight is over, comrades will terminate the relationship.

I seek continually to understand these roles, to avoid crucial mistakes of judgment. I will know one from the other by listening, as people tell me what they are here for. I will slow down and listen. When they tell me what makes them tick, I will believe them!

Do
_____

I do treat confidants, constituents, and comrades accordingly.

Reflection 32

Before I try belonging, I calculate the benefits and drawbacks.

You

God created me to need other people, both intimately and socially. I recognize that like tends to attract like, and group familiarity provides me comfort and security. I also recognize that groups tend to be exclusive, and elevate group members into a special category.

Is belonging, for me, more about social status, giving back, helping, or networking? I consider the organizations I belong to and how long I've been involved with each of them; knowing the types of organizations I tend to join reveals a lot about what is important to me.

Before I join any group, I think it through and do a personal cost-benefit analysis to determine what's to be gained, compared with what I will invest.

Do
_____

I do weigh the costs and benefits of joining or remaining in any group.

Reflection 33

Before I pursue any relationship, I will first know who I am and love myself.

You

I will never feel better about myself simply because of the club to which I belong or the group I join. I must not expect to receive something from my affiliations that they cannot begin to provide for me.

I may fool everyone in the club, at church, or wherever, but I know all of my insecurities. The only way to feel good about myself and to grow in confidence is to know who I am and love myself. This begins with self-education and personal exploration.

Until I fully understand my real motives for my associations, I will set myself up for disappointment with any group, any relationship. First, I get clear about the person I want to become and who I need to associate with to become that person.

Do ⎯⎯⎯⎯⎯⎯

I do examine my own motives for affiliating with any person or group.

Reflection 34

Before I ask what an organization can do for me, I ask what my unique contribution can be.

You

I have to be very deliberate about where I commit to serving. The challenge is not discerning good or worthy causes, but discerning where I can effect the most positive change through my contribution. I must ask myself before I join: What can I uniquely contribute? Many organizations and institutions want my time, money, and talents. But only a few need what I have to offer that no one else can contribute—my passion, my talent, or my ability to enable that makes me irreplaceable.

Many people can donate time and money. Many can set up the chairs for the meeting or make cookies for the reception. I won't join if I cannot add something new to the group.

As with any other major decision in my life, I will take a good long look at the dynamics of my involvement and my motives for joining a group. If I examine what I will gain and what I alone can contribute, I am much more likely to enjoy my affiliation.

Do

I do serve where I can make a unique contribution.

Reflection 35

Before I seek true intimacy, I begin with the decision to love.

You

I acknowledge that sex without intimacy is running away from intimacy, engaging in the most intimate of acts, yet disengaging and blunting emotions to avoid the pain of connecting in a healthy relationship. True intimacy requires transparency and vulnerability, honesty and acceptance, and trust. True intimacy requires deciding to love.

I admit I have sometimes tried to find ways to divert myself from the hard work and frightening pursuit of real intimacy.

I open myself to the possibility that intimacy is not romance or even passion, but comes from sharing daily life and personal realities with a committed person.

I will not overlook the small details of the connection I feel with other people. I will not wear emotional condoms or focus on protecting myself from heartache. I will risk vulnerability—not casual sexual interaction—for the hope of love.

Do _____

I do forgo casual sexual interaction and pursue true intimacy.

Reflection 36

Before I consider a partner, I affirm that the person does not have to be my equal, but rather balance my strengths and weaknesses.

You

I don't just want to dance alone in life. No matter how successful I am in every area of life, I find that I long for a spouse.

Instead of hoping for an ideal that doesn't exist, I am willing to discover what it means to love another human being, flaws and all. I would like to be in a healthy marriage. I would like to share my life. I will consider who I am missing, looking past at the next person coming through the door, rather than at the person right in front of me.

While I will never "settle" for someone, I will look for someone who complements my strengths, rather than shares them. I don't have to marry someone who's my equal in every way. The reality is that no one is totally anyone else's true equal. The beauty of relationships is people who complement each other entering into the shared space of intimacy, with commitment.

I am willing to reconsider someone I may have dismissed because I saw them as beneath my level of success. I am not better than anyone just because I have more education or money, and he/she is not better than me if they have more. I allow myself to meet our individual points of need and strengths. I will not be ashamed or feel threatened by this person's strengths, because they will only make my own strengths sharper and stronger. I will be confident enough in my own strengths to love and respect my complement as an equal.

Do _____

I do seek a partner who complements me.

Reflection 37

Before I pick a life partner, I affirm that I can't choose by looks or by what others think.

You

I have to ask myself, Do I want to marry someone who fits my profession or my personhood? I must share my private life, my internal world, with this person. What works for me in public may not work at all in private. I must stop picking out people like I'm shopping for a watch. If I go about looking for a life partner this way, I will always be disappointed. There must be substance to the relationship. In moments of crisis, when sickness gnaws at me or my family, when hard times descend like a shroud over the finances, I need someone I can count on. Love is more than a seasonal occupation.

Differences cannot be ignored, but neither should they inhibit or limit me in my choice. The other people in my life will always have something to say about anyone who varies from their preconceived notion of who is acceptable. People may try to annul a union that works for me but doesn't work for them, whether it is on racial, financial, social, educational, or religious grounds.

Do
_____

I do open myself to the partner who is right for me.

I do go into relationships knowing what I want.

Reflection 38

Before I risk love, I recognize that it becomes harder as I get older.

You

Deciding to love gets harder as I get older. I've lived long enough to have been disappointed, heartbroken, and jaded. I am sometimes even cynical about trusting other people and about the prospect of finding someone to share my life with. It is more and more challenging to risk and so much safer and more comfortable to resign myself to loneliness. I examine myself and admit whether I am more than contented with my single life and have no desire to marry and raise a child, or whether I am lonely.

As I get older and have more roles and responsibilities draped around me, I honestly examine myself to see whether I crave a meaningful, passionate relationship more than ever. Do I want someone to love me for who I am and not what I do or what I provide financially or materially? Do I long for someone to give me permission to let go of all I cling to so fiercely in the daylight hours of my public persona? Who will walk beside me when my hair is silver or gone? Who will travel with me when I retire or stand by my bedside when I enter my final illness?

Do

I do take the risk of loving.

Reflection 39

Before I carry old hurts, I drop them, knowing they keep me from being open to new love.

You

I have had relationships that didn't work out. But carrying around old hurts and resentments keeps me from being open to future relationships.

I am mindful of Dr. Maya Angelou's words: "Courage, you have to have courage to love somebody. Because you risk everything, everything."

Do

I do have the courage to let go of the old and accept the new.

Reflection 40

Before I can find what's missing, I have to acknowledge loss.

You

I long for a heart's companion but it's tempting to think, When I have so many other areas going for me, why get hung up on a relationship? I know in my heart that the right relationship would make my life complete. I am being honest with myself and not pretending that something isn't missing. I'm missing having a relationship and I want it; I won't ignore it or allow others to talk me out of it. I won't mask the truth from myself. I know what I want. I really ponder this question: Am I in the right environment to find the kind of mate I'd like? I take the risk to look around me and see where I need to be to find the partner I seek and make the right affiliations to facilitate the kinds of relationships I want to establish.

If you're already married or in a relationship, instead of

the above, this is your affirmation: I'm already married or in a relationship, but I need to create the intimacy that's missing or recapture the love I once knew. The more history we spouses have, the more joy as well as the more pain we have experienced. All relationships have growth areas that need pruning and fertilizing.

I commit to secure what's missing relationally in my life and make the necessary decisions to love boldly and passionately.

Do _____

I do acknowledge my desire for a partner or a better relationship.

Reflection 41

Before I choose based on looks, I remember that what I see might not be what I get.

You

Dating doesn't always tell me what it will be like to be married. A Facebook profile doesn't tell me how someone really looks, let alone how they will treat me after the first date is over. Some details simply cannot be ascertained until I experience the fullness of the situation. When you first meet someone, consider their manners, how they treat the restaurant staff, what types of interests they have, if they share your spiritual beliefs, if they show interest in what you have to say.

Someone may look perfect from a profile online, or seem like my soul mate because of the incredible compatibility determined by our twenty-nine personality trait tests. However, there is no substitute for real interaction over time. I will be cautious about online dating sites and community chat rooms, knowing that people can easily impress online.

Do
_____

I do not base relationship decisions on anything but authentic interaction over time.

Reflection 42

Before I have an affair, I remind myself that it will not provide me an accurate picture of the person.

You

Stolen hours, spent devouring each other emotionally, sexually, and intellectually, are not a foundation for a good relationship and marriage. Affairs exhilarate the senses. Good marriages are made of the commitment to real passion, maintaining a sense of mystique and intrigue, ongoing creative romance. The feeling of an affair and marriage are not the same and they will never be. Instead of looking for satisfaction outside of or instead of marriage or looking for a new mate, I'd best commit to finding a marriage mate, not a date, or, if I'm already married, renew my commitment and look for ways to recapture or introduce romance and depth of intimacy in it.

Do

I do honor marriage.

Reflection 43

Before I get emotionally involved with someone, I will listen closely to what this person self-reveals.

You

I admit to sometimes ignoring what didn't work, and looking only at what did work, what we had in common. I have been blinded to the warning signs that could have circumvented a bad choice. I have turned a deaf ear to the warning, missed the glaring issue that eventually lead to the demise of the deeper, more fulfilling relationship I want and need. I have failed to listen to the warning signs.

I will learn how to listen. And not just how to listen to others, but how to listen to myself. I will learn to read the fine print of meeting, dating, and interacting with someone; I will heed the red flags. I will listen to the voice inside. I will process all the data and listen to my gut.

Do

I do listen to the voice inside me about what I hear.

Reflection 44

Before I think I can change the other person, I recognize that as foolish.

You

I have no right to take on another human being as a project. I cannot assume the role of savior and try to be anyone's redemption. If I have a "need to be needed" complex, I cannot allow that need to influence my relationship choice. The power to change must come from within each person, not from their partner. If others saw a change in their spouse, it wasn't coming from their influence on their spouse. It came from within the person who changed; that person desired to change.

I leave the salvation of people to God. I do not pervert the romantic into the redemptive. I must not mistake myself for God in someone else's life. I must allow the Almighty to work in my life, and to work in the other person's.

Do _____

I do not take on a partner as a project.

Reflection 45

Before I begin my research, I first examine myself.

You

I have blind spots that tend to obscure my view of my prospective partners, and I either tarnish them with my own fears or else paint a glossy veneer on an unstable surface. I begin to examine the expectations I set based on my own self-awareness. The place I begin my research is at home. Before I can begin to scrutinize the other person, I must recognize my own limitations and motivations for the relationship.

Because self-image has so much to do with effective communication, I work on seeing myself as valuable enough to deserve love and attention from the other person. I form a boundary that I will not compromise. If this foundation of self-worth is not in place, I become so grateful for any kind of love that I ignore the price.

I do not choose to live with blinders on rather than to

confront the truth. I garner the courage to ask and answer questions that reveal who I really am and what I really want. I don't want to be seen as arrogant, but I will remain confident. I open my mouth wide, take a deep breath, and start the process. I do not sulk in silence and secretly ponder issues that could be resolved by simply asking, "Why?"

Once I look realistically at who I really am and what I desire in a healthy relationship, I am ready to expand my research—to the other person.

Do
_____

I do examine my own limitations and motivations.

Reflection 46

Before I commit, I research.

You

I will not be embarrassed to ask questions that will determine whether I should spend my precious time with someone. I will become savvy at adding meaningful dimensions to my discussions, to learn what is below the surface of my prospective partner. I will ask the hard questions and observe important areas with a critical eye. I will avoid repeating my past mistakes, as well as the other person's. I will not entrust my heart—not to mention my resources of time and money—to someone without first ascertaining their suitability. I will ask questions and examine the other person critically but in a gentle, respectful, caring way, not offending the person or losing the chance at a relationship.

I will not move into ultraimportant relationships without real insight into the person to whom I'm committing.

Do

I do ask the hard questions before I commit.

Reflection 47

Before I commit, I will become relationally literate.

You

People use the same words and mean different things.

In my conversations, particularly before our discussion has ended, I will say, "Let me tell you what I heard so I can see if that is what you meant." I will make this a practice. This interaction alone can open me up to a richer line of communication with others.

When I am asking serious questions or broaching important areas of concern, my demeanor will be one of a student wanting to know more about a subject of great interest. It will not be an interrogation, a condemnation, or an indictment. I will make it a way to gain some insight into our hearts and minds. Aside from gaining facts, I am also learning how to communicate with someone important to me. I am learning my partner's language, knowing such relational literacy will serve me well for years to come. Feeling the freedom to ask my questions and to answer someone else honestly forms a crucial foundation for how I will communicate moving forward.

Do
_____

I do listen to what my partner is really saying.

Reflection 48

Before I love, I am realistic about motives and intentions.

You

I open my eyes along with all my senses to see the other person. I want to "hear" what is being said beyond their words. I read their motives, their mannerisms. I pay close attention, because answers are formed by more than the words. Even if my partner and I are not good at talking about our deepest selves, I am deductive as I piece together clues about who the person really is. I pay careful attention to the body language, as well as the manner in which they respond. Defensive and evasive answers, sitting cross-armed, and failing to make eye contact could all be signs that they aren't being 100 percent truthful.

I stop. Look. Listen. It's the formula for a wise decision about how I will gather necessary information about my prospective life partner.

Do

I do pay attention to what may be unsaid as well as to what is said.

Reflection 49

Before I get too involved, I investigate.

You

I may feel like a snoop, a spy, or a private detective, but I will do the due diligence to find out all I can about my prospective partner's past, present, and future. I will casually ask around to those who know them in different roles, do some internet research on the person, and google them. It's public information, not illegal or immoral or unethical. I will not be offended if the other person is doing the same research on me.

If I find information that disturbs me, I will ask them about it, or give the person a natural opportunity to inform me. In the case of a discrepancy between what they've told me and what I've discovered from another source, I must determine the truth.

It is important to get to know the family. The family,

friends, and colleagues have vital information as to how he or she thinks or operates that is very important for me. I'll ask to see the places where this person grew up, favorite areas, and meet people who have known them throughout different life seasons, to get a clearer sense of their character. I know it's essential to discuss physical health issues and fiscal health.

Investigating my potential spouse will feel uncomfortable but cannot be overlooked. I will let them know by saying, "I'm excited about our affection, but I do want and need to know you better." I will earn their respect by not being sneaky. I will be forthright and honest.

Do
_____

I do investigate and ask about anything that troubles me.

Reflection 50

Before I get engaged, my mind, emotions, and imagination should be engaged by my mate.

You

I can be bored by myself. I don't need a boring relationship. One of the most overlooked areas in relationships is stimulation—the kind of stimulation that emerges from the other person's ability to engage my mind, excite my emotions, and ignite my imagination on a wide range of life topics.

As time passes and the years go by, we will become intimately acquainted with each other's ways to the point of predictability. I must be and look for a person who finds ways to keep self-improving and then bringing that to the table of our relationship. Reading, learning, cultivating friendships, interests, and hobbies are ways to stay engaged by life. Stimulating people stimulate each other. I must know how to develop an interesting life without depending on a shared life.

Lifelong learning and stimulation are the hallmarks of a healthy person and a healthy relationship.

Do
———————

I do work to keep myself and my relationship stimulating.

Reflection 51

Before I get bored, I pay attention to what and how the other person celebrates.

You

I want to celebrate and be celebrated by the other person in my life. I want room in our relationship for feeling good and enjoying each other on a daily basis. As the novelty wears off and boredom threatens to set in, I need to know how the other person faces the gifts that each day and each season provide.

I want to be where I'm celebrated and not tolerated. Being celebrated does not mean a party. Celebration includes the ability to comfort and console me through the dark days or to notice the sunsets, the smell of spring in the air, or the laughter of a child skipping rope on the sidewalk. It is the ability to remember birthdays, offer encouragement, and give gifts unconditionally. To celebrate the joys of life even amidst its bitter downturns is a priceless quality.

Do _____

I do celebrate my mate and expect to be celebrated in return.

Reflection 52

Before expectations kill my relationship, I examine whether they are unrealistic.

You

My expectations are often based on my past experiences. Adjusting expectations will help alleviate disappointments.

A vast difference exists between who I am versus who I present myself to be, between my ideal self and my real self. I do not meet and marry the ideal, but the real. The ideal projections of both me and my partner can create expectations that counter the reality of our relationship once the masks are off. We both overpromise and underdeliver. We expect our relationship to go a certain way; it veers from our trajectory; and we end up offended, by the other person, we think. But it was really our expectations.

I will minimize my expectations or at least adjust them to a realistic framework: to expect nothing more than I'm willing to give. Because expectations are nothing more than future resentments, I avoid those resentments by allowing the other person to give freely. I rob the individual of blessing me from their heart when I have unhealthy expectations.

I will be blunt and ask the other person their expectations from a relationship with me. And tell them, in kind, what I expect.

Do
_____

I do honestly state my expectations and ask my potential spouse to do likewise.

Reflection 53

Before I count on sexual chemistry, I talk honestly about sex.

You

I need to discuss my idea of a fulfilling sex life before I marry, not after. I feel awkward about this, but I can make it fun and lighthearted. I start by telling my partner what great sex looks like to me. We cannot build our relationship around our sexual chemistry, because only about 10 percent of our time together will be spent in the throes of passion. I cannot ignore the sexual dimension of our relationship, either. Having sex does not equate to being intimate, but building intimacy usually results in a mutually satisfying sexual relationship.

I won't wait to ask the HIV/AIDS question until I'm in the heat of the moment when passions flare. I will make sure we each ask and answer the question honestly. (And if I haven't been tested recently, I will be.)

Do
_____

I do candidly discuss sexual issues in our relationship.

Reflection 54

Before I learn or share secrets, I commit to not judge.

You

Everyone has secrets, no matter who they are or how virtuously they live. These may be family secrets dealing with substance, domestic, or emotional abuse. They may be personal secrets dealing with past relationships or present addictions. They may involve a criminal record, children from another relationship, a past abortion, or an unrevealed adoption.

I listen without judging the other person so that they feel safe enough to share truthfully. I want them to accept my secrets without criticism or condemnation. I set a tone where we both are willing to confide in each other, dirty laundry and all.

Being direct and frank about such matters can also prevent the future keeping of secrets and simmering of shame from the past. In my investigations, I want to know all, but I must be willing not to judge the person. I also need to divulge my own secrets. Reciprocity is key to building and maintaining trust in a healthy, life-sustaining relationship. Whatever the secret, it must be dealt with before I can have a healthy, lasting relationship built on solid ground.

Do

I do allow the other person to share secrets, and I disclose mine with an open heart and mind.

Reflection 55

Before difficult issues surface, I will bring them up for discussion.

You

Sometimes I avoid asking certain questions because I am afraid to hear the answers; once I hear the truth out loud, it may confirm my worst fears, and then it's harder to move forward, pretending I don't know the truth.

It's not easy for me to ask about sexual history or a criminal past. The answers could be embarrassing, but it will be more uncomfortable later if the secrets are suddenly revealed in an unpleasant or public way, or if I hear the information from someone else.

There are significant issues in my past that my partner should know, and vice versa. Everyone has secrets. It's better to reveal them up front than to have them found out later. I will bring up the subject. If I reveal something difficult and my partner walks away, it's better that I know how they feel up front. I won't go into marriage in the dark about important issues. I will create a safe atmosphere for us to be honest. I will be sensitive. I won't judge but will understand and listen.

If I am not willing to be a safe place for my partner to be transparent, I am not ready for a relationship. If I decide not to pursue a relationship, I must still be a good friend, at the very least, and respect the other person's privacy by not sharing confidences.

Do
_____

I do create a safe atmosphere for both of us to be open about our past.

Reflection 56

Before I dismiss differing points of view, I will learn healthy ways to approach disagreements.

You

I admit I do not have a clue about understanding and communicating effectively across the barriers of my own perspective. Honestly, I am looking for a version of myself, yet am often attracted to people who are as much like me as water is like vodka. (They are both clear and wet, but the similarities end there.)

People with differing points of view make life interesting, make conversation stimulating. I need to learn ways to approach disagreements and differences that widen my opportunities for relationships or help my partner and me make our marriage work. I commit to being respectful of my partner's ideas and experiences, and to making others feel free to express their feelings and be who they really are—without fear of judgment or condemnation.

Do
_____

I do work to bridge differences and create lasting bonds.

Reflection 57

Before I love, I must make time.

You

Because finding time for each other is one of the greatest challenges for today's couples, I must make bonding time. After spending so much time ignoring the clock as we date, flirt, and get to know each other, I must not suddenly cram the romance into neat half-hour slots on my Microsoft Outlook calendar! We need quality time to talk. We must continue to take time to get to know each other. It takes a lifetime to get the rhythm right between two people. This is not a matter of love but of finding our "normal."

Do

I do make the time to get to know my partner.

Reflection 58

Before I commit, I will learn how to share.

You

Each partner has equal responsibilities in most relationships now, but we have not been taught how to share. We share the space with people we love, but factors like gender and personality differences make it difficult to share effectively.

I admit I am not one of those people who easily shares with others. I can be argumentative, rebellious, or selfish. Every day as I work with my mate to find our rhythm together, I will listen, liberate, and lavish the other person with the freedom of unconditional love, as I learn to share.

Do

I do share with my mate.

Reflection 59

Before I shut a door I will not be able to reopen, I will stop and think.

You

Before I divide, separate, or otherwise loose myself from what I have, I will be sure to think things through.

I'm afraid of regretting. I don't want to make a mistake by letting a person go who should be there, but how do I fix what was acceptable at one point but isn't anymore? How do I amend some things that I said or did, now that I realize they were wrong and unjust?

If I feel that I need more space, I will make sure what I perceive as a need for space is not really a need for intimacy, for direct communication, and for change.

I have to respect what I have even when I enter a place of discomfort and pain. I don't close a door on love just because it squeaks a little and has a hole in the screen! I won't shut a door that I can't reopen when my season of frustration is over.

Do
_____

I do think things through before shutting a door I can't re-open.

Reflection 60

Before I marry, I create a charter for our marriage that allows for change and growth.

You

If I lose my willingness to change, I have lost my willingness to survive. This includes humility and the ability to admit my mistakes and ask for forgiveness.

Before I marry, I must create in myself an openness to change and an understanding that much correction will be needed for what I will face with my spouse. This attitude is our charter for how we will operate in our new country of togetherness.

We do not make permanent decisions over temporary circumstances. We regularly recalibrate our relationship to ensure that the decisions made at one stage of life now fit the growth and maturity of the present.

Do _____

I do work with my mate to redraft our charter as I grow.

Reflection 61

Before I receive forgiveness, I offer it.

You

We all make mistakes. As human beings, we are all flawed. Perfection only exists in God our savior. Recall Jesus's words: "Father, forgive them; for they know not what they do" (Luke 23:34, KJV).

It is perfectly normal and healthy for me to feel angry, wronged, or disrespected. But the caustic emotion of bitterness is not healthy. I cannot let myself become bitter.

Grudges spread and invade our healthy emotions. Forgiveness conquers bitterness.

I can always rely on God for forgiveness no matter what I've done. When I am tempted to withhold forgiveness, I remember my need to be forgiven and reconsider. I treat my loved one with the love, respect, forgiveness, and mercy I'd like.

Do

I do forgive as I want to be forgiven.

Reflection 62

Before I wed, I accept the challenges and difficulties of marriage.

You

Happy endings take a lot of work. I enter into marriage with expectations of conflict and challenges that require a tremendous amount of work. I am willing to be flexible. I release the need to be right and to win. I want a stable, long-lasting relationship.

Do

I do the internal work that will make me a good spouse in the difficult days of marriage.

Reflection 63

Before the stronger personality arranges the relationship to suit them, I make the required effort to ensure equity in our marriage.

You

Whether I am the stronger personality or not, I understand how one partner's selfishness disrespects the other person. In a marriage, each spouse deserves equity and liberty.

I must be mature enough to admit when I am wrong. I risk humility to correct my mistakes.

Our relationship will not last because we weren't ever wrong, but it will last because when we were wrong we found the invincible will to correct it and the grace to endure whatever it takes to survive it all together. Families are never perfect, but that doesn't mean that with honest conversation and cultivated respect I cannot find a way to make love and life good.

I free my relationship from the shackles of false expectations and limited perspectives. My beloved and I negotiate new boundaries, new borders, and new policies. Our wedding vows have the power to bring about an incredible emancipation from our loneliness, selfishness, and isolation.

Do

I do what is fair in our marriage and am willing to correct mistakes.

Reflection 64

Before I risk something new, I accept that fear is normal.

You

Like everyone, I sometimes get nervous. It's a normal part of the process of doing anything new. That is the nature of crossing a fresh threshold into the exhilaration of a new experience. I face new experiences with some degree of angst. But I say, Feel the fear and do it anyway. As I work through relationships and marriage, I muster the courage to do something I've never done before and accept that anxiety is normal.

Do

I do feel the fear and but I do it anyway.

Reflection 65

Before I relate fully, I learn the value of faith.

You

God has a way of putting me in a place where I have no choice but to move from the safe center to the uncertain edge of a new experience.

I admit, I would avoid making the change or facing the edge if I could.

In the titillating, terrifying, gut-wrenching, soul-tingling feelings of this "stuff" of relationships, I learn the value of faith and the fuel of prayer. I activate both as I face the uncertain.

Do

I do access the power of faith and prayer in my relationship.

Reflection 66

Before I give in to my anxieties, I respect what is at stake.

You

I am scared. This whole idea of building a relationship the right way, a new way, is scary to me. In the nervous moments, the sweaty palms moments, when the tension in the room is thick and exhilarating, respect for the stakes often raises the degree of anxiety. My respect for the gravity of the decision of marriage makes me a little edgy and uncertain, prayerful and careful.

But the only way I can avoid these nerve-racking feelings is to always play it safe by sticking to what is easy and familiar. How boring! I don't want a nonprogressive life, never to venture beyond where I started.

Do

I do expect some anxiety before marriage because the stakes are high.

Reflection 67

Before I avoid making a change, I will risk moving from my safe center (comfortable place) to the uncertain edge of a new experience.

You

Some people have to be pushed over the edge or they will never go beyond where they were born. I affirm I'm not one of those people. Not anymore. To stay where I started is to die without growth. I may never have taken a chance and discovered new dimensions to my identity and interests if relationships hadn't forced me into action. Relationships change me in some way. Relationships push me into a great and new experience in my life. I believe God pushes me into these wonderful possibilities that I would never embrace if the decision were entirely mine. While any committed relationship, especially marriage, has its challenges, one of its blessings is that it brings me to the edge.

Do

I do embrace the possibilities when I am pushed into a new experience.

Reflection 68

Before I give up, I affirm that the sky is the limit!

You

I set my relationship goals high so that we cannot achieve them on our own, so God is needed for us to fly!

Even if this is my second or third or umpteenth attempt at a successful relationship, I won't give up. Scripture tells me to be cast down, but not destroyed (2 Corinthians 4:9, KJV), which reinforces the truth that I can fall but not fail. And, just because I feel myself falling does not mean that I failed. There is a second chance, and a third, that is inherent in the process of success.

I was not made to play it safe. The sky is the limit! I move into my destiny. I will then pray, "Heavenly Father, what's next?"

Do

I do take a risk, and find out what is next for our relationship.

Reflection 69

Before I buy a home, I affirm that it is more than a house.

You

I want a place where I belong, more than just a place to which I return after work, eat a meal, and sleep. I want comfort, convenience, and a style that says something about who I am. It will be a retreat, a safe place, a sanctuary that enables me to recover from the blows of life beyond its doors and that feels like a home to family and welcoming to friends and guests.

The attitude of the people living there, my attitude, creates these qualities. Money buys me a house, but only my life there makes it a home.

Do

I do create a true home.

Reflection 70

Before I decide to have children, I acknowledge everyone is not cut out to be a parent.

You

I examine my reasons for wanting to have children to reveal whether or not I am ready to nurture a family—at once the most rewarding and most difficult and dynamic task I will ever undertake. I may realize that perhaps I am not now, or may never be, ready to have children. Not everyone is meant to be a parent.

Motivations to want children vary, and if I have them, I want to do so for the right reasons: because I want to build a family unit and feel the desire to selflessly support another being into a mature, well-rounded adult.

Reasons that are less than desirable—ones that are likely to result in heartbreak for me and my child—are such reasons as "I want someone to love me," or "My partner wants them."

I will do some serious soul searching before proceeding down the road to becoming a parent.

Do ─────────────

I do examine my motives for wanting children.

Reflection 71

Before having a child, I make internal and external preparations.

You

Having a child means my life is no longer my own. My home is no longer my own. As a woman, even my body is no longer my own. It may be difficult to make room for a child, both literally and figuratively, in all dimensions of my life, but it can help me become less self-centered and more compassionate. When I no longer think of only myself, I grow in unique ways that do not occur in any other relationship.

The child bridges the practical, everyday aspects of life with the eternal privilege of being God's facilitator for bringing another soul into existence. If I become a parent, I must learn to address both of these areas.

If I do not feel joy at the thought of parenting as a lifetime commitment, then I need to accept this reality and not pretend otherwise. I will not deceive myself into thinking that I'll just "grow into it" after the baby is here. Parenting is 24/7 for the rest of my life! A baby is not a cute accessory that can be carted around for display. Having a baby is like dropping a beautiful stone into the calm pond of my life—it will ripple into every relationship and settle far beneath the surface.

Do
_____

I do prepare myself inside and out for this new life.

Reflection 72

Before I parent, I will commit to counter the negative messages that bombard children.

You
_____

Children face a world that is full of negative influences today, no matter how much parents try to protect them. I must be their moral and spiritual compass.

It will be my job as a parent to counteract negative influences by setting an example for my children, teaching them the right values—to work, to save money, that our lives are not meant to revolve around acquiring status-symbol possessions.

When I become a parent, my kids will always be watching me. What I say, how I act, and what I do are the model for the persons they are likely to become.

Do _____

I do commit to being the moral compass for my children.

Reflection 73

Before I accept childlessness, I can be a role model to a child.

You

Raising children is not just a job for parents. I can "parent" children by having an impact on their lives, caring for them, and taking an interest in them. No matter who I am, or where I go, whether I have children or not, some young person needs my support, my guidance, or a kind word of encouragement that could change the direction of a life for the better.

I can volunteer for a children's organization, become a Big Brother or Big Sister, give time to an after-school program or a church organization, or reach out to a child in my family—a niece, a nephew, or a young cousin. The world can be a hard, confusing, and lonely place for a child, even for children who have a parent or both parents. A strong, encouraging relationship with me could make all the difference in the person they turn out to be, and can fulfill some of my desire to parent.

Do
_____

I do reach out to children in need.

Reflection 74

Before I use the word "divorce" lightly, I will eradicate it from my vocabulary.

You

Using the word "divorce" to threaten, manipulate, and cajole a spouse into doing what you want them to do is never healthy for a satisfying, functional partnership. It is emotional blackmail. If I continually threaten divorce it's clear that I view marriage like a suit of clothes to be tried on, altered, and adjusted; worn for one season; and then discarded for the next dress on the runway. Often divorce is unnecessary and becomes a lazy way out of a stormy season that will only thunder and crash around me louder when I'm suddenly alone. Divorce is never easy and neither should contemplating it be easy.

Do _____

I do not treat divorce lightly or use the possibility as a threat.

Reflection 75

Before I accept biblical grounds for divorce, I consider whether it is the correct course.

You

"'I hate divorce,' says the Lord God of Israel" (Malachi 2:16, NIV), making God's perspective on the subject plain and clear. Similarly, Jesus says, "It has been said, 'Anyone who divorces his wife must give her a certificate of divorce.' But I tell you that anyone who divorces his wife, except for marital unfaithfulness, causes her to become an adulteress, and anyone who marries the divorced woman commits adultery" (Matthew 5:31–32, NIV).

I see clearly from these Scriptures that my Creator did not desire me to enter into such a sacred oath and leave the back door open for a convenient exit strategy. I must also consider Jesus's words in Matthew 19:8: "Moses permitted you to divorce your wives because your hearts were hard. But it was not this way from the beginning" (NIV).

I must keep in mind that just because Jesus says that unfaithfulness provides grounds for divorce doesn't mean that it *necessitates* divorce. Where my marriage is concerned, I must not rush to judgment if mercy can heal the relationship.

Do _____

I do not rush to judgment and divorce.

Reflection 76

Before I remain indefinitely in a bad relationship or marriage, I consider divorce, as a last resort.

You

I do not deny it if my relationship is lethal, for reasons ranging from health issues (contracting diseases) to safety (spousal abuse). Such may necessitate separation and dissolution of my marriage.

I have to face it if I am trapped in a sexless, loveless, or violent relationship that is destructive. God does not expect me to stay in the marriage at any cost. Sometimes divorce is the only way to put an end to a season of pain, suffering, and loneliness that is far worse than the aftereffects of the separation.

I examine my "deal breakers"—those offenses for which I know that, for me, there will be no going back. For some this point is infidelity; for others it's substance, verbal, or physical abuse, or serious dishonesty. I have to decide for myself what this point is for my marriage. If I did not discuss it with my potential partner before we got married, I will do so now.

Do _____

I do not stay in a destructive situation if divorce is clearly the only solution.

Reflection 77

Before I look outside to get what's missing inside my marriage, I examine myself.

You

When something is lacking in my present relationship it is tempting to look to another person for what is missing. But the truth is I must examine myself. Before I have the affair, I recognize that a perfect person does not exist. My spouse, a flawed, work-in-progress human being—just like me!—can bring most of what I need to the relationship, but not all. The rest is up to me. I must guard against becoming more and more aware of what I'm missing and starting to look, subtly or not so subtly, for something I already possess. There are no perfect people or perfect relationships. The reality of intimacy is that we only grow close to each other when we struggle, fail, forgive, persevere, and press on together.

Do _____

I do guard against relating in inappropriate ways with someone outside my marriage or relationship.

Reflection 78

Before I give up hope on love, I relearn the art of knowing.

You

The art of knowing the other person is fundamental to love. Individuals often try to figure out the other person, put them in a box, and label them for the rest of their lives. Knowing someone is a progressive art, not a static science with immutable data. I must view the other person as a mystery that requires ongoing scrutiny and lifelong learning. The Bible tells me that a man and a woman should dwell together according to knowledge (1 Peter 3:7, KJV). I must be willing to revision my partner, who may not be who I thought, but neither am I.

Do

I do allow room for both of us to evolve, revolve, and resolve!

Reflection 79

Before I give up hope on love, I relearn the art of listening.

You

I must practice *the art of listening* a regular basis. I will cease reciting monologues, preaching sermons, or making speeches without leaving room for a real conversation. I will slow down and hear the other person's language, without being so busy trying to get my point in and outscore in the fight. I will listen for solutions and places of negotiation, listen with an open heart instead of a closed mind.

Do

I do learn how to communicate at a new and deeper level.

Reflection 80

Before I give up hope on love, I relearn the art of waiting.

You

I must not underestimate *the art of waiting* in its ability to restore beauty to my relationship. This art combines patience with perseverance and can be excruciating at times as I bend but refuse to break. While I wait for the new love to grow or the old love to heal, I need patience. I know that those who wait on the Lord shall have their strength renewed. God's timing produces a healing deeper and richer than anything I can force to happen.

Do

I do exhaust every option before severing the relationship.

Reflection 81

Before I give up hope on love, I relearn the art of forgiving.

You

The art of forgiving is the hardest art for me to master.

No one stays married to anyone without some forgiveness involved. God doesn't stay with me without my asking forgiveness. If I don't practice forgiveness in the little things, it makes it that much harder to extend and receive grace during the crisis moments. The art of forgiveness requires letting go of perfection and performance and grasping hold of grace and gratitude.

Do

I do forgive.

Reflection 82

Before I give up hope on love, I relearn the art of openness.

You

The art of openness requires me to remain vulnerable, transparent, and willing to trust again. My heart is clenched and tight after pain or rejection, a reflex mechanism in my soul, a way I protect myself subconsciously. This is the state where I love the person, I still come home at night, but I am braced, no longer present in the moment. In marriage, I must turn off this mechanism. Otherwise I will close my soul. I have closed myself for fear of disappointment or hurt. Marriage is a covenant of openness consummated by sex, which removes all barriers and celebrates the joy of there being nothing between the two people. It is difficult to attain and maintain such intimacy, both emotionally and physically, after betrayal and disappointment. If I have lost the closeness, I can get it back if I'm willing to relax my soul and open my heart toward the other person.

Do
―――――――

I do practice the arts of knowing, listening, waiting, forgiving, and opening my heart.

Reflection 83

Before I divorce, I consider the consequences.

You

Divorce has consequences. Divorce carries unseen ripples of regret and tremors of second thoughts for the rest of my life. Orphaned memories will continue to survive although I have been ripped away from the partner who helped make those memories. Heartache will exist between in-laws; I will lose friendships and intimate family connections; many I care about will be forced to choose sides.

Marriages build equity over time like a property growing in value year after year. The collage of intimacy that had been artistically assembled by the life we shared will painfully peel away. Am I ready to throw away all that equity and start all over? It will take years to get to the same level.

Before I sign on the dotted line and terminate my status as a married individual, I look at all facets of the relationship along with my motives. I do everything I can possibly do before initiating the termination of a relationship.

Do _____

I do everything I can to preserve my marriage.

Reflection 84

Before I despair over a necessary divorce, I affirm that it can be a catalyst for rebounding and repositioning myself.

You

Just because I hooked up with someone doesn't mean that God put us together.

I'm grateful that there is life after divorce. The marriage afterlife can become a season of starting over and loving myself and meeting my own needs. I can rebound from the trauma of a life reconfigured and reposition myself for the remaining years. I can recover without dragging the baggage of my past into the next relationship. People I respect and admire have endured it and gone on to make sizable contributions to the world. Getting a divorce is not the eulogy to my life and my capacity to love. It can be a catalyst for rebounding and repositioning my future.

Divorce is not a death sentence, but I must examine my life with honesty, candor, and wisdom.

Do
———————

I do rebuild and rebound if I must divorce.

Reflection 85

Before I quit, I will self-examine.

You

I sometimes want to quit my life. I admit this secret fantasy of running away and leaving everything behind, starting over in another country, culture, or relationship. I sometimes feel sick and tired of everyone sucking the life out of me without putting in anything in return. I want to disappear and never look back.

It's obvious that I might leave the circumstances behind but I'll never escape myself.

Before I quit anything—my job, my marriage, or my life—I commit to think about *why* I want to leave and where I want to go next. I will seek a clear perspective on what I'm releasing and what I'm moving toward. I'm doomed to repeat the past if I don't examine my prior choices.

Do _____

I do think about where I want to go before I leave something behind.

Reflection 86

Before I quit, I will think about why I want to leave and where I want to go next.

You

Sometimes I have quit the wrong things at the wrong time. I have relinquished the dreams that would have sustained me on my journey in favor of the dreams of others. Pleasing my parents, conforming to others' expectations, and taking the most convenient opportunities that came my way have caught up to me. I feel a slow-burning rage.

Sometimes I have been so afraid of change that I now need to quit something in order to make room for the next season of my life. I may need to quit my present job, relationship, or church situation in order to make room for my next career, person, or fellowship. I vacillate between boredom with what I have and my fear of future uncertainty. I will re-

vive those unrecognizable longings that have been languish-
ing deep in the bottom of my heart.

Do
_____

I do examine my prior choice because it helps me to know
what I'm leaving and where I'm going.

Reflection 87

Before I "settle," I call forth my dreams.

You

I have dreams that I have buried prematurely that God now wants to resurrect in my life—my education, starting my own business, pursuing a relationship, or expressing a creative talent that I have had to stifle.

I know that all of my dreams won't come true. In the daily grind of living and working I have learned to be realistic. However, I call forth my dreams. I make a conscious choice to believe they are possible, and I rise to the level of faith such a transformation requires. I face my past disappointments and recalibrate my expectations. I dare to hope and silence the internal critic. I dare to hope and ignore the critical chatter from others in my life who are either incapable of supporting or unwilling to encourage me in my endeavors. I dare to hope.

I grieve the past wrong choices I've made. I forgive myself as well as others who have discouraged me.

I can celebrate hope, with true appreciation for new chances to dream.

I am willing to face the facts about my dreams and how I have changed over the years. I consider how my dreams can bless others as well as fulfill my own purpose. I must allow my dreams to evolve just as my life has evolved and I must be willing to see them transcend my own happiness.

Do

I do dare to resurrect my dreams.

Reflection 88

Before I quit pursuing a dream, I realize I can't afford not to dream.

You

As I get older, I think of dreams as a luxury I can no longer afford. Dreams have been replaced by "more serious" concerns. The realities and responsibilities of life prevent me from dreaming, but maybe those "realities" are really excuses or fears that if I try to do something different, something I dream of doing, I will fail. I have convinced myself it's better to quit while I am ahead, or at least comfortable.

This kind of pessimistic attitude keeps me stuck in life. Giving up on dreams is like giving up on hope. Hope and dreams are all I really have. Some dreams are not meant to come true, yet many of the dreams I give up on, with a little love and care, can be resurrected, like Jesus.

Do _____

I do not give up on my dreams.

Reflection 89

Before I break through to the next level of success, I will nearly fail.

You

People who have achieved great things in life are usually no more gifted, intelligent, or privileged than I. They simply have learned to lean into their mistakes and persevere through them to the next level of challenge and expectation. I'll win if I don't quit. I have never seen a quitter win, because there is simply no way possible to win if I quit. But if I don't give up, I can win.

Something that starts out understaffed, underfunded, and underperforming can still succeed. I risk moving out of my comfort zone. Success is not found in safe places.

Do

I do take the risk of failure.

Reflection 90

Before I obtain dreams worth having, I will have to take risks.

You

I must overcome my fear of heights and be willing to risk failing at the next level. I will feel the fear and try to flutter. I must have the tenacity to withstand the fluttering stage of building my dream. If I believe in it, then I'll fight for it, one battle at a time.

If I see no way humanly possible for my dream to succeed, that can be a positive because it keeps me humble, willing to seek and accept help from others, and on the lookout for divine intervention. Dreams worth having should not be attainable on my own strength—such are merely goals. Dreams must be worthy of the talent, time, and tears I pour into them so that success is so much larger than I could ever have delivered on my own.

Before I quit, I must overcome my fear and be willing to risk failing at the next level. Feel the fear and still try. I revive my dreams and refuse to give them up to past mistakes and present regrets. Everyone is tempted to quit at times, to give up the fight and just accept mediocrity. But the next time weariness weighs me down or trials temporarily trample my dreams, I will ask the Lord for my strength to be renewed.

Do _____

I do ask for new strength and press on in the face of risk.

Reflection 91

Before I resolve conflict, I understand the pain of the other person.

You

In resolving conflict, I listen to the pain of others. Real truth isn't held in the pain of one side—even my side—but also understanding the pain of the other. The compassion for one doesn't negate the need of the other. I facilitate healing for myself and others.

If I truly want to escape the hold those I am in conflict with have on me, I must understand their pain. One-upping "the enemy" is not winning, only delaying the healing process.

Do

I do seek to understand the pain of others even when I am a victim.

Reflection 92

Before I fight, I must select where and when to direct aggression.

You

As I enter the fight, I must choose where to direct my energies of aggression. To heal any conflict, I have to give up the need for revenge, retaliation, and being right and fight for the greater good. But this choice brings its own pain. Sometimes I have chosen to repeat the injury rather than initiate the healing of forgiving and understanding another's pain and fear. That brought temporary gratification, but, in the long run, the war continues when the healing could have been under way!

Life presents challenges that require personal warfare to survive. But in order to channel my energy and resources into the right battles, I must exercise patience, wisdom, and faith in God's goodness. The next time my blood pressure escalates and my temper flares, the next time I dismiss someone's offer of help or assume that finding a solution is a lost cause, I will examine my motives before I fight. Sometimes I must fight my own inclinations rather than fight those around me!

I look carefully to realize who I'm fighting. Maybe I am fighting the wrong enemy. Maybe the fight I must win is not an external but an inner one.

Do

I do pick my fights wisely.

Reflection 93

Before I put my "fight or flight" instinct to good use, I use mature judgment.

You

Discerning when to fight and when to walk away is crucial to maturity. Which instinct is more refined in me?

When I fight, I must be willing to struggle for a solution that's larger than my own agenda. Aggression is not always a bad thing. My fighting instinct can be put to good use. When I feel passionately enough about something to fight, I emphasize its importance. My anger, frustration, or feelings of powerlessness can be healthily transformed into the fight of perseverance, determination, and achievement.

Do

I do fight for those things worth fighting for.

Reflection 94

Before I fight, I determine whether I love fighting more than winning.

You

Some things in my life conditioned a fight-prone personality. The good Lord did not create me to be passive and hide, avoiding conflict. God gave me the gift of anger and the fuel of adrenaline. Without such tools, predators would pilfer my possessions, and bludgeon my self-esteem. I have to fight to love, to live, to survive.

But before I fight, I must think deeply to understand whether the spoils justify the fight.

I think through which fights to engage and which to avoid. I realize that some people are not as interested in results as they are in conflict, and am not led by people who love to fight. They don't want a solution as much as they want to continue the battle. They don't love winning—they're in love with fighting!

I also ask myself, Is this me? Is that my truth? Have I fought so much over the years that I am stuck in fight mode? Am I locked in a perpetual state of anxious alert?

Do _____

I do not stay stuck in fight mode.

Reflection 95

Before I disengage, I accept that conflict can be an opportunity for true love and grace to flow.

You

People don't have to agree on every issue to be agreeable. Conflict is often a real opportunity for the true love and grace of God to flow. Love doesn't mean I am weak or that I have changed my stance when I believe I am right and fair, but I often have more of a template for conflict than I do for peace. I will welcome the opportunity to talk to those with whom I might disagree.

Do

I do look for opportunities for peace in the midst of conflict.

Reflection 96

Before I dismiss those who think differently than I do, I remember I might learn something from them.

You

In the interest of peace, I must learn to speak and to interact with people who think differently than I do. It doesn't mean that I have to change my views or my message, but I need to change my method if it is hate-filled. Much can be accomplished when I'm willing to engage in real dialogue.

I must show love, not hostility. I must unite, not divide. Talk, not shout at people. Respect them as equals. Truly exchange ideas. Look for opportunities to work together. Crossing lines into territories where I risk rejection isn't easy. I will be a peacemaker. Powerful peacemakers are crucial to conflict resolution.

Do ─────────────

I do talk to and listen to those who might differ with me.

Reflection 97

Before I fight, I distinguish friend from foe.

You

Sometimes when I am used to being attacked, if I am not careful I can fight the very one who has come into my life to help me. Sometimes I lack the ability to discern when and where it is necessary to engage in conflict and when peaceful solutions are possible, and miss the blessing God had sent my way.

There is a big difference between being a coward and being careful. God often sends me help in unlikely places from unexpected sources, but when I fight quickly I often destroy the provision intended to enhance my opportunities. I will cultivate the ability to draw strength from unusual resources. Past pain sometimes makes it difficult for me to accept current caring. I will put away my sword and open my heart, so I am not fighting those who could help me. I know

that sometimes divine help comes in an odd uniform and
that my next place of affection, affirmation, and affiliation
may not come packaged in the way I expect it.

Do
———————————

I do expect help from unexpected sources.

Reflection 98

Before I run, I realize it is usually the easy way out.

You

If I am always running away from problems, then I will never mature into the person God designed me to be. And if I keep facing toxic relationships and abusive situations, then I haven't learned when to leave.

Maturity necessitates that I know how to discern and decide when to run and when to figure out how to make something work. I admit that sometimes it can be too easy for me to run. Sometimes I run when things are going too well; I'm terrified to taste intimacy. I fear it won't last.

Other times I don't want to face the hard work of loving someone when the going gets tough. As long as the romance and infatuation last, I'm fine. But as soon as communication breaks down or trust fractures, then I'm out the door.

I will no longer make flight into an art form.

Do

I do stay and face the hard work of loving someone.

Reflection 99

Before I waste time, I take flight from those who do not want to or cannot engage in a mature relationship.

You

Sometimes I accept tentative relationships without my expectations being met. I invest time in relationships that go nowhere. I am no longer willing to spend my time this way. Even someone who sincerely cares for me but lacks the relationship skills and personal maturity to fully commit can no longer warrant my time. I cannot counsel an unwilling partner through the process to a place of commitment. I will waste no more time or emotional energy trying to overcome a reluctance to commit. We both must be willing and able to work through these issues.

Do

I do let go if need be.

Reflection 100

Before I leave, I fight for the love I want.

You

I realize that lovers must also be fighters. I have to fight to love. When I know that there is love, I need to dig in and work through conflict. Relationships require me to take a stand. I have to fight not to lose my ability to love. I may have to fight through the grief of a terminal love experience to open my bruised heart again. I might have to fight off bombs of depression and the urge to become cynical and bitter. I am not a person who gives up on love, becomes indifferent, if a relationship doesn't happen quickly and conveniently. I understand that people who make love work, work at love. I do not consciously or unconsciously slip into a state of avoidance and seek convenience rather than the complexities of working through the issues and seeing the relationship through.

Sometimes I have to walk with the pain of a relationship until it works, or I know that I am right to walk away from it!

Do _____

I do fight for the relationship I want.

Reflection 101

Before I make assumptions, I respect differences and learn from others.

You

I live in a world that doesn't teach respect for differences or tolerance of others' perspective. But I will not lose my ability to engage in dialogue, to listen, and to remain open-minded. Otherwise, my personal life will show the erosion of negotiation. "My way or the highway" is wrong because it precludes understanding differences and seeking common ground.

I must spend time with people who are different from me. When I only interact with people who look like me and think like me, I have no checks and balances to avoid extremes and to provide wisdom. If I only have friends who vote like me or worship like me, I have no sense of *the* world, only *my* world. How can I make more frequent connections with those who are different from me—in schools, on the job, and in church? What will force me to look for points of unity rather than to sink into the all-too-easy states of homogeneity or divisiveness? It is easy to see how we are different, but I have to look deeper for what unites us. Then I will be a real lover of people and stronger in my relationships.

Do ─────────────

I do look deep for the things that can unite me with others.

Reflection 102

Before I let our differences destroy the relationship, I learn to find the common ground.

You

I tend to become attracted to people who are different from me. Then what attracted me to the person in the first place later disgusts me. I know that people were meant to balance each other by attracting people whose strengths may be our weaknesses. Together, as a result of our differences and distinctions, we complement each other.

But in order to enjoy that beautiful union of diverse tendencies and ideals, I must learn to stand up to the pain of readjustment and the tendency to avoid doing the hard work of making things work.

The next time I think it is easier to leave the person I am involved with, I will remind myself that understanding only comes when I "stand under" a real desire to know, to love, and to comprehend the person, embracing the uniqueness of who they are.

Even the best relationships require negotiation, deliberation, and a lot of work. Romantic relationships require that I celebrate differences and find common ground.

Do
_____

I do embrace my partner's uniqueness and understand our differences.

Reflection 104

Before I risk, I don't gamble on the important issues of my life.

You

I am not someone who has a gambling problem, but if I take risks in important areas of my life, repeating the same mistakes—in relationships, at work, with my kids—I might as well have a gambling problem.

While I cannot avoid taking risks in life, I can only be effective if I discern whether what I do is an investment in the future or a gamble in the moment. The word "faith" is not a religious license to gamble. I cannot write checks on faith, knowing that the funds are not in my account but hoping that they will somehow miraculously appear before the check gets processed. I cannot marry on faith, hoping and believing that the other person will change later. I cannot accept a position that I know I am not qualified for because I have faith that I can learn what I need to know later.

This is not faith. It's gambling. Just because I want something doesn't mean that I should claim faith and overextend myself to go after it. Faith without works is dead, just as works without faith limit me to my own abilities. Faith plus works produces investment into my purpose.

Do

I do not use faith as an excuse to gamble with my life.

Reflection 105

Before investing for the long term, I must educate myself to make wise decisions.

You

Risk produces fear and uncertainty. However, I realize that I can live with the consequences of my choice. But before I choose, I reflect, discern, accept responsibility, and I do my due diligence—my research and development. I seek the counsel of many wise individuals who know me and my calling, and study. I have faith, but I also do the hard work of gathering data and listening to others. There is risk but no gamble.

Gambling is built entirely on chance, while risk creates a chance to make my dreams a reality.

Life will always require me to take risks, but I must discern which risks are worth taking and which will short-circuit my long-term goals for short-term payoffs. If I only think about what feels right in the moment, my weaknesses will undermine me. I keep my eyes on the prize of my larger goals and greater calling if I am to make the right decisions at the right times.

Do

I do know the difference between gambling and wise risk taking.

Reflection 106

Before I waste time, I affirm that time can never be recovered.

You

When I waste time in dead-end relationships, I have lost priceless moments that can never be recovered. When I remain in a career that numbs me and stunts my growth, I lose a part of my true identity.

The most common result of wasted time involves regret. I admit I have wasted time. Out of fear of rejection, I didn't speak up. Out of fear of failure, I didn't step out. Out of fear of being alone, I didn't tell the truth. I've invested quantities of my time in endeavors that offered no return on quality.

I want to make the most of my decisions. I will never again lose sight of the fact that time is our most limited resource and can never be recovered once it is spent. I can go bankrupt and recoup my money. I can endure a scandal and rebuild my reputation. But my time passes and is gone forever.

How much younger I would be if I had back the time I wasted. Have I invested time in dating someone who didn't have what I was looking for? Have I made a bad decision to marry?

Time will always be one of my most precious commodities. Before I invest it in someone or something, I define what the return should look like. I am running out of time.

Do _____

I do consider the potential for return on my investment of time.

Reflection 107

Before I allow my name to be used, I investigate carefully.

You

I am careful not to gamble away the integrity of my identity, not to have my name misused. I take precautions when vouching or someone for standing up for someone.

Names are vitally important in the Scriptures. Jesus said that if I receive the disciples that come in his name, then I have received him. He also said, "Whatsoever ye shall ask the Father in my name, he will give it you" (John 16:23, KJV). God told Abraham that his name would be great.

The power of my name is better than an impressive title or an inherited fortune. When my name is great enough, I don't even need money—I have the inherent integrity of my character.

Do _____

I do defend and protect my good name.

Reflection 108

Before I take a leap of faith, I must draw a line between faith and foolishness.

You

The defining factor emerges from what I place my faith in. Jesus taught me to have faith in God. There is a difference between faith in the One who orders my steps and has a design-logic that's so certain I can rest in it, and faith in believing what I want to happen will transpire if I squint my eyes and imagine it enough times in my head.

Visualization is a powerful motivator and performance enhancer; however, I must have my higher priorities as the lens through which I see my achievements. Faith is only powerful when placed in God. My own faith is not powerful enough to actualize my desires.

Starting with faith in God, I still cannot win big if I do not cultivate some simple inner characteristics, get away from luck-living or gambling for the things I want and need. Real results require study, research, action, and yes, again, faith. I understand that real progress is not made by closing my eyes and wishing.

Once I have done the research, developed inner disciplines, and chosen wisely, I can live without fear. The Vegas style of living is not for me. I will still win some and I will still lose some, but I proceed without fear. Even the wisest decisions don't always turn out well, but they are far more likely to do so than wild gambles. Take the bitter with the sweet. An occasional loss isn't a sign I am living a Vegas life.

I move into my destiny, valuing myself and my time, my opportunities and my influence. I live my life without fear of regret.

Today is the day that the Lord has made. God has given it to me. What I do with it is my gift back to my Creator. The Almighty has given me the talents and the time that I have. I am highly favored. As I live wisely, God gets a return on creation—God's investment in me. I make it a big win for myself and God!

Do _____

I do walk toward my destiny in faith and without fear.

Reflection 109

Before I perform, I envision.

You

The time for preparation and planning has passed. I have completed the preparation needed to begin an extraordinary performance. I envision myself going through the intricate motions of my most exceptional performance. From beginning to end, I mentally visualize each detail that must be included, each step or stride, each note or line that I will include in the execution of my role. Like watching a movie of myself in an Olympic-medal or Oscar-winning performance, I perform a mental dress rehearsal to prepare for the actuality of my success. I envision myself doing what I have decided to do.

Do

I do see my extraordinary future.

Reflection 110

Before I act on my decisions, I have to "see" my success.

You

"I've done it!" That meaning captures my present state of preparation, motivation, and actualization. My future requires action now. I've done the due diligence of research and development, of seeking counsel from my confidants, and of preparing those around me for change. But I still may experience fear and find myself immobilized.

The missing ingredient may be my ability to see myself succeeding, regardless of past mistakes and future challenges. I must be willing to trust my gut, take the necessary risk, and seize opportunities. I can be tempted to paralyze myself because of the possibilities. Deferring my decision until other people or circumstances decide for me is a decision. Living passively is a choice even if I'm unwilling to acknowledge that I've chosen it!

I put aside all excuses. I am not afraid to act. Talent applied to skill produces unequaled success. Talent is my God-given gifts. Skill is my hard work, practice, and preparation. I recognize opportunities when they present themselves. I take the steps, one after another after the next, to bring my best life to living color.

My decisions have the power to shape my life one day at a time. I can anchor my life in intelligent preparation. I make sound decisions. I am like a tree planted beside living waters, as the psalmist calls those seeking God's righteousness (Psalm 1). I water my tree with self-forgiveness and nourish it with good relationships. With the sunlight of God's grace shining down on me, I can reach for the sky, and grow beyond my wildest dreams.

As I finish this last page and close this book, I will take a small step toward giant success. My prayer is: God, I will look within and unleash the wellspring you have placed within me. I allow you, Creator, to flood my life with the joy of your Almighty blessings. I commit to become all that you, dear God, have created me to be. I advance confidently in the direction of my dreams that please you, by practicing the power of positive decision making on a daily basis.

Do _____

I do take action to become all that God intends me to be.

Acknowledgments

Before I do something as challenging as writing a book like this, I count on the contributions of so many others to enhance this collaborative endeavor. My decision was predicated on the incredible support, encouragement, research, and resources of so many talented individuals. Thank you to my staff and team members for freeing up numerous hours in my schedule, allowing me the time to reflect, recollect, write, and revise. I pray their decisions to commit to my ministry and my mission will never be ones they regret in any way.

No publishing partnership can function at maximum capacity without the dedication of key leaders and contributors. With this in mind, I find my gratitude for my family at Atria Books only continues to grow. Thank you to Judith Carr, Carolyn Reidy, Gary Urda, and Christine Saunders for catching my vision for this book and breathing it into life with a fervent passion for excellence. My appreciation for the efforts of Michael Selleck and Larry Norton on behalf of this book continues to grow. Sue Fleming's participation in the process of producing this project greatly enhanced its quality.

A special note of gratitude to Malaika Adero for her editorial expertise, flexibility, and grace under pressure. I'm also grateful to Dudley Delffs for his feedback and input on this book.

Jan Miller and Shannon Marven at Dupree Miller & Associates continue to amaze me with their passion for my work and their relentless commitment to the very best solutions. I cherish their wisdom, friendship, and shared vision for where my message can go. To Dr. Phil McGraw: thank you for your support, guidance, counsel, and camaraderie as I stretch and grow into new possibilities.

Finally, to my wife, Serita, a wordless thank-you of eternal gratitude for your decision more than two decades ago to join me on this joyful adventure. Your love, patience, support, and encouragement enrich every area of my life and our life together. To our children, I offer a father's loving appreciation for the ways you continue to grow into maturity and responsibility that comes with making adult decisions.

List of Topics

Your Own Reflections

5